Happy Easter
1974

Gentle Harvest

GENTLE HARVEST

Poetic Moods and Memories
Of a Woman's Life
by Florence Jacobs

Selected and arranged
by Dee Danner Barwick
Illustrated by Muriel Wood

 HALLMARK EDITIONS

Printed in the United States of America.
Library of Congress Catalog Card Number: 75-102165.
Standard Book Number: 87529-027-2.

Contents

GENTLE HARVEST

The space within my heart is small,
And this is how I know it:
Soft winter twilight through the tall
Pine boughs can flood and fill it all,
A star can overflow it.

Love and Marriage...
A Life Together

I SENT MY DREAMS

I sent my dreams beseeching
  Through Heaven's golden glooms:
"Please, God, a little cottage,
  And love to light its rooms."

But God is very busy
  And therefore gave me you,
Who one by one and slowly
  Make every dream come true.

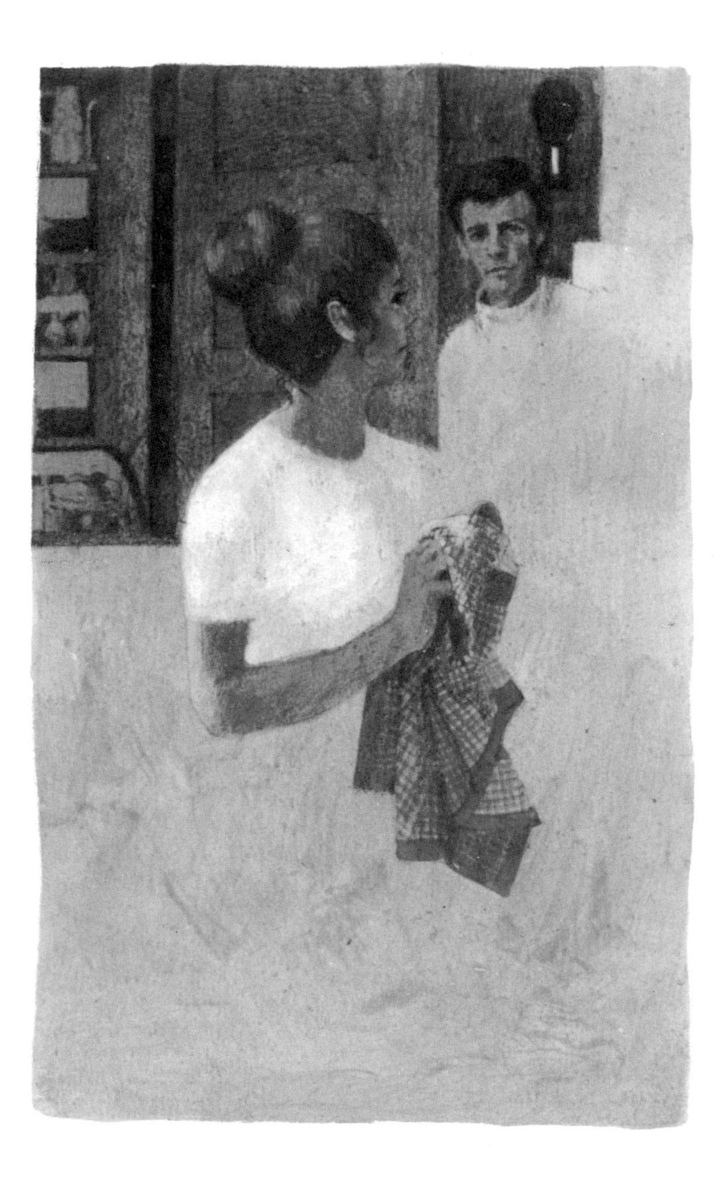

COMMUTERS' SPECIAL

All day I function happily enough
in second gear, say, with some little part
idled. A joke is tucked inside my heart
for later sharing; any newborn buff
kitten, new-blossomed tree, cannot be relished
fully till night, certified and embellished
by love's companionship.

Dusk settles down,
a half-moon climbs, the cars roll in from town,
incidents rise to mind like cream, life quickens,
the cat perks up, the pallid gravy thickens
and browns, rich odors crust a casserole,
you come through the door, and I am whole.

ALL I EVER WANTED

All I ever wanted,—
A little, little house
With sunlight in the kitchen
And chambers deep in boughs;
To get up in the morning,
Crisp bacon, shape a theme
From outline of new silver,
Blue cups and yellow cream;
To whisk the rooms to neatness,
Dispatch the work along,
And all the time be humming
Gay snatches of a song;
To run out on the doorstep
For one look at the lake,
And pull a spray of lilacs
To cool me while I bake;
Perhaps in middle morning
Sit where the breeze draws through,
And write some singing verses
Out of my love for you;
To press my newest muslin
And start to pay a call,
—The joy of being a landlord,
And locking doors, and all!—

Sit with the other women,
Gossip a bit, and sew,
But all the time be conscious
Of that deep inner glow;
To hurry home from calling
Because it's after four,
And make your favorite shortcake
From fruit the garden bore,
Then comb my hair out softly
The way you like it most,
And listen for your footsteps
While garnishing the roast.
—Swift days, shot through with loving,
With laughter gay as light,
And walks of courtship glamour
When moons are high and white.—
And then before the fire,
From close against your chest,
To whisper you that secret
Which glorifies the rest.

FROM UNDER A GREEN THUMB

When it's hot as Hades,
a nice cold cut
served in the shade is
my own choice . . . *but*
the peas grow ripe
under rousing heat
and perhaps we gripe
but it's peas we eat.
Comes the perfect time
for a coastal trip. . . .
Now the corn is prime
so we let 'er rip,
stay home to can
what would soon be spoiling—
and the pressure pan
isn't all that's boiling!
Tomatoes flourish.
I spend the day
begging the parish
to cart away
this fruit of our labors,
this mad surplus . . .
who's knocking? Neighbors,
with some for us!

THE NIGHT BEFORE MARRIAGE

Tomorrow, when I come to you,
I put within your hand
body and heart and soul, as who
but women understand?

My lover, make me wholly yours
in all the ways there are,
so a sweet bondage more endures
than either lock or bar;

So that I never leave your breast
to dream of other things,
but find in you my end-of-quest,
my comfort . . . and my wings.

OVERNIGHT CABINS

Stop before dusk, laying out household goods
to make a supper of savory native foods
(Cat Chat strawberry jam, the long brown loaves
baked in a Gaspe oven).
                    Walk in birch groves
or a hay-sweet meadow, till ocean mist rising damp
under a full moon, hurries us back to camp.
Watch while the little houses of Ingonish
are lighted, the stars above it, and make a wish
that the road to Canso may circle!
                    Pack again, starting
out in the fresh summer day, nostalgic at parting,
at leaving behind a background already dear . . .
a little of home, of marriage, of love shared here.

THE SOLITAIRE

Summer and winter, day and night,
dreams come true by the clear white light
of this treasured symbol, this fiery splinter
from love's own heart.

Through summer or winter
the setting's a forecast, a golden rumor
of blessing to come.

And winter or summer
precious memories of courtship stay
locked in its beauty, night or day.

FASHION NOTE FOR EITHER SIDE OF MARRIAGE

Some tender dusk between May
and September
have this to remember:
a delicate gown,
cobweb-sheer, garden-colored,
cloud-soft, flowing down
to slippers like petals beneath
its wide hem;
your waist for the stem.

(Time enough to be sensible,
competent, agile . . .
it is not reprehensible,
now, to seem fragile;
now, with the young body curved,
the young flesh
supple as cherry blow,
hair showing fresh
glints of a bird wing.)

Just for this hour,
enchanted, exquisite,
look like a flower!

MEIN KAMPF

The place is a bedlam
  of boiling and baking,
washing and ironing,
  marmalade making,
then a knock on the door
  is the world and his spouse
and they want to come in
  and sit down in the house!

Tomorrow's bright dawn
  offers leisure for dusting,
all windows are polished,
  all pipes freed of rusting;
the rooms are as fresh
  as a holiday card,
and every last caller
  camps out in the yard!

THE HAPPY MOOD

It's lovely, and it's *mine*,
and I shall not expose it
to the wind, the weather
or the world's comments;
in a green-edged corner
of my heart I'll enclose it
with mist and moonbeams . . .
and it *needn't* make sense!

THE WALK,
Thanksgiving Afternoon

On the edge of day
I come down from the pond.
Far-away leaves
burn a witch-fire blue,
there's a rising chill
and the early dark . . .
and a wide field still
to be gotten through . . .
something small and furry
moves in the night . . .
but the yellow spark
of our kitchen light
streams out beyond . . .
and I hurry, hurry
from things that scurry . . .
from those who stray . . .
toward the safe home eaves,
and the fire, and you.

In the Country

DAY IN THREE DIMENSIONS

Here in the old house
are all my times;

not bound to any chronological year,
I am every age at once.

Running up the path under the maples
is my childhood,

while old age waits in the rocker,
in the other room.

EVENING WALK

Come along, then, but leave behind the talk
about plans, pressures, even memories;
come without hurry or aggression, walk
easily, lightly, take for what it is
this different world, this quiet, muted place
of silent meadows, starlight, shadows, space.

Open your mind to beauty. Recognize
what a new, subtle pigmentation lies
in landscapes with the color blotted out
and only form left (pencilled curve or stout,
smudged, sooty masses), nuances of line,
jet-black or charcoal shadings, a design
varied from clustered cedars to the trace
of steel-bright pool, the sapling's silver lace.

Speak, when you must speak, gently, so a thrush
will not break off his lovely liquid call
from the deep woods, so loon and water, all
night voices carry on the still air.
                    Hush,
an owl. . . . Lean here against the pasture bars
and listen to the earth talk, and the stars.

SUMMER NIGHT

The nicest way of neighboring
Is in a little town
When folks are done with laboring
and dusk has settled down.

We all go out to weed a bit
before the light is gone;
The menfolks see the need of it
and start to mow the lawn;

One leaves his grass and comes to talk,
one calls across the hedge,
Then all together take a walk
along the river edge.

And when the summer stars are thick,
each woman carries home
A scrap of news, a household trick,
a pot of special loam.

THE LAST WORD

"If it was *mine,*" folks often say,
"I'd cut those bushes all away,
trim out the wild plums, have a neat
cleared space around the garden seat."

It isn't theirs. And let's admit
green tangles border where we sit
in summertime, but I *like* green,
while those who talk have never seen
the loveliness plum branches bring,
the sheer delight, one week of spring!

THE SNOWPLOW

The snowplow comes crashing by
soon after midnight,
shattering a silence which has been
too still, too white, fifteen hours long;
rousing slumberers with the clatter of its gears,
its backing and turning,
the shouts of its crew,
breasting drifts like a red-eyed behemoth,
leaving behind a wide, smooth course.

And all along the route watchers by sickbeds
draw breaths of relief . . .
now a doctor can get through;
members of Lodge committees stop worrying
over salads turned soggy
and cake gone stale . . .
the Anniversary dinner will not have to be postponed;
students from high school in town smile
and go back to sleep . . .
no absent marks for them tomorrow;
a newly engaged girl hums under her breath . . .
the mailman again in the morning, with overdue
letters;
pregnant women relax into peaceful rest . . .
let their hour strike now whenever it will!

THE SKY WATCHER

She lives with the weather—while muffins brown,
searches the elms for a thunderous crown;

between dusting parlors and waxing floors, often
wades down a March field to see how snows soften;

scrubbing or ironing, still must peer forth . . .
is the wind making up? shifting from north?

Never draws curtains, wouldn't be able
to tell if a full moon rides on the gable;

slips out at bedtime where hill-pasture bars
afford a last check on the state of the stars.

WOODS CHILD

Quiet is her native element
As air the oriole's, or a wild green
Covert the fawn's, silence that makes a screen
For tentative and secret moods.
Content,
Like the small spotted fawn
In the deep covert,
She feels the stillness put out tendrils, spread,
Gives herself to it and forgets to dread
A sudden overt
Clamor, a violence of discord rushing
In fierce assault upon the spirit, crushing
All tender growth, the shy buds.
Now she loses
Even those bruises,
Continuous harsh sound leaves . . . she expands
To a full stature, blossoms out, her hands
Still on her lap, curved like the sickle moon,
Wide open to accept the evening's good;
Shadows of twilight wood,
A single vireo call, distant, lonely,
Muted until it only
Underlines
The windless hush among these ancient pines.

FIRST THINGS FIRST

Spring work accumulates in careful lists,
clean closets, wash the blankets; housewives rally
their forces.
                    But the elms are yellow mists,
pale golden powder; crooked willows lean
above the wild dark water's headlong sally;
the poplars thicken to a lacquered screen;
crab apple fingertips keep rosy tally;
and my whole business for today consists
of starry-eyed narcissi in a green
pool, of green waves that surge along the valley.

EMINENT DOMAIN

I own the field—although a crow disputes
my title with his loud protesting squawk
from border elms, some pretty saucy talk
comes from a squirrel, and a gray owl hoots
all right to dispossess.
                    Strawberry yield
will never reach my lips while robins swoop
on every crimson ball; the young deer troop
and trample hay crops down.—I own the field?

THE FULLNESS THEREOF

"Oh, you should travel,"
They tell me, "should go
Where Lombardy poplars
Rise row upon row;

"Where Africa's desert
Lies white as a stone,
Or Nippon's small gardens
Are rosily blown."

"And what should I gain
If I left my own town,
And the shore where my birches
Hang whispering down?"

"Why, you would find beauty,
And love, and life's smile,
And not sit and stagnate
Within a square mile!"

"Well, here are my trees
In a nimbus of green,—
If that is not beauty,
Pray, where is she seen?

"And here underneath them
Came love and its dole,
To warm me, and sear me,
And recast my soul.

"And after, a wonder
So golden and high
It gave me the keys
To the earth and the sky.

"Beauty, infinity,
Sorrow and strife,
Both kinds of loving,—
What else is in life?"

WEATHER REPORT IN BASIC ENGLISH

It rained,
then it snowed,
then it blowed. . . .
No,
it rained
then it blew
then it snew . . .
oh,
what it did was to *rain*, together
with other weather.

PLAN FOR A SPECIAL DAY

When everyone's away
some morning in the summer,
I shall get up early,
smooth back the quilt,
carry out my coffee
to drink on the doorstep,
wrapped in a housecoat,
naked of guilt.

All the summer morning
I shan't hear the doorbell,
shan't read a letter
nor answer the phone;
but drift through the orchard
casual as bluebirds,
scrawling little verses
against a flat stone;

and all the summer evening
wander in the starlight
down a misty meadow . . .
I all alone.

STORMY NIGHT

The wild gale rose; black rivers poured
   on misty glass, and pine
boughs twisting off like orchard grass
   took down the power line.

We got the lamps out. Yellow light
   lay soft as primrose bloom
across the kitchen, spread its pools
   half through the sitting room.

Each corner rounded in with dusk,
   dressers loomed twice as tall,
and once again my childhood walked
   in shadows on the wall.

WITH THE LILAC HEDGE AND THE LOCUST TREE

"How can I be lonely outdoors?" said she,
"with the lilac hedge and the locust tree,
young woodbine growing,
a wild stream flowing,
and all my friends, all talking to me?

"A silent house, that's different," she said,
"The creaking timbers a century dead,
an empty chair,
a voice not there,
and the long, long memories inherited.

"But here," she said, "there isn't an hour
barren of life! Birds sing, clouds flower
from the wispy, thin
scuds gathering in,
to the sweet warm drops of an April shower!"

The Beauty That Is Nature's

KINSHIP

The mighty hills give some hearts aid—
but as for me, my solace lies
less in eternal peaks and skies
than in an oak whose summer shade
is mortal, too, a transient thing,
vulnerable; whose trunk is scarred
by storms; which still can face the hard
white winter out and look toward spring.

SPECIAL DAY

The loveliest spring morning!
  Blue iris by the brook,
A deep, deep sky, and four blue eggs
  Tucked in the elm tree's crook! . . .
So special, even, that the moon
  Stayed up awhile to look!

THE SOUND OF GLORY, THE COLOR OF PRAISE

Good sober black the choir wears,
the dark-clad worshippers intone
their psalms.
                    A brilliant morning flares
outside—leaf, petal—summer's own
amber and gilt in a green bowl
stained orange where the oriole
soars, soars, and carries up to Him
rich thanks for richly budding limb!

MORNING, OVERCAST

Cross the path lightly, heedful of the rare,
Thin, satin-textured morning . . . let each move
Be tenuous and subtle, in a groove
Of slow cloud, languid river . . . turn with care
So that no startled robin takes the air
In orange flight to shatter this pure scale
Where tones of leaf and grass descend from pale
Boughs to the darkness tranquil waters wear.

The misty sky is blurred into a cool
Background; no tulip opens to intrude
On this veiled hour, this exquisite gray mood
Whose pulses never left the poplar screen. . . .
See, therefore, that your gown is apple-green,
Your heart as quiet as the shadowed pool.

COMPULSION

I must go out this morning, chart
blossoming orchards, learn by heart
one rosy peach, a single pear
lacing white boughs across blue air;
wander through meadows, overwhelm
with contours of a wineglass elm
my spirit; cool myself in dark
backgrounds of cedar, turn and mark,
dazzled, how dandelions spill
a sheet of hot gold down the hill;
memorize tulips, velvet-lined.

(I might be in a town, or blind,
some Maytime, need to close my eyes
and let this tide of glory rise.)

THESE VARIED SHOWERS

These varied showers spilling down
over a little country town
are all so lovely! May's bright spears
pricking to bloom the sleepy years . . .
October's gentle mists that shield
harsh outlines of the harvest field . . .
soft cotton flakes or brilliant frost
worth all the icy winter's cost . . .
one day in June, a warmer snow
drifting from every poplar row . . .
and then along each autumn lane
the downpour of a scarlet rain!

RAIN IN AUGUST

The cool gray curtain of the rain
shuts softly down, and closes in
behind its slanting silver-thin
tissues, a winter peace again;

no sound comes through except the brush
of light folds over velvet grass
where misty garments flutter, pass
with healing in their blessed hush.

THE FIELDS COME IN

All day, this time of year, the house
Is full of movement. (Not that creaking
The boards make, when an old stair tread
Remembers footsteps of the dead
On frosty nights; nor dry leaves squeaking
Against dry shingles.)
                    Now a mouse
Takes shelter from the early cold
In the snug space between the boarding;
Out in the well house squirrels scold;
A chipmunk scuttles back and forth
Along the ridgepole, briskly hoarding
His food against the time of north
Winds, and vine hangs thick with birds,
Fluttering, twittering.
                    Soft words,
Light rapid motion, curving round
So delicate a plane of sound,
It overlaps but does not merge
With ours. . . . You will see go by,
Out of the corner of an eye,
A swift gray shadow; *feel* a surge

A breathless rush you cannot hear,
Quite. . . . And another world is near,
Minutely scaled, clandestine, just
Beyond our senses but alive,
And only furtive as it must
Be to survive. . . . . . .

MIDAS TOUCH

A golden year! In fall the tamaracks
spread their antique bronze on pasture lot
and upland; oaks turn russet; ripened stacks
yellow in cornfields; sunsets apricot.

In spring the catkins and the lemon-pale
forsythia, the birches' sulphur-green
powder along a brookside; in the swale,
new plantains, delicate young alder screen.

SIDE CROP

A farmer harvests beauty all the year:
he prunes a rosy orchard slanted up
some hill whose angle brims with sunshine, clear
as Pearmain cider rising in a cup;

he mows white stars; his sepia-toned shocks
deep russet pumpkins frame and emphasize;
then in the wintertime he hauls home blocks
of frosty moons, of delicate pale skies!

ICE STORM

The midnight gale is spent—a windless morning
Glitters across this meadow where each fence,
The final twig and cedar bough, condense
Beauty to silver lines, pale stars adorning
A rainbow world so delicate one breath
Surely dissolves it.
Silence pure as death
Builds up, is ripped apart by sudden pistols
As ancient willows yield their crusted length
To the still weight, the cold and ruthless strength
Which underlines these frail, translucent crystals
With devastating force.
All over town
The old and brittle limbs come crashing down.

JANUARY REVERSAL

My garden, that was buried deep
in aromatic snow
Last May, now decorates its sleep
with crystal cherry blow.

POINT OF VIEW

Some people need their marvels
To be spectacular—
A rose in winter gardens
A strange and eerie star

Beside the sun at midday.
But as for me, I go
Deep in a constant wonder
That life and death are so.

SAP TIME

All day the eaves thaw
in a warm March sun,
and yet the wind blows raw
from snowdrifts piled
where northeast sides of barns
stay winter-wild.

Sunsets are still.
The wind drops, and the long blue
shadows spill
their freshets under trees
skeleton-stark.
By midnight it will freeze.

The morning maples bud
with jays . . . with pails
to catch a precious flood;
through every spout
spring's essence, clear and thin,
comes seeping out.

A Woman's Memories

ECONOMY

She braids the past in beautiful
rag carpets for her floor—
Father's gray homespun, scarlet wool
Great-aunt Lavina wore.

Nothing is wasted, thrown aside
from memories or gear:
nine decades of rich life provide
a background for this year

wherein she smooths the feather bed
of century-old down,
and touches, quilted in the spread,
her mother's wedding gown.

INTERLACED WITH WONDER

Blessed with two childhoods, mine and hers,
the space between them often blurs . . .

I can't be sure who caught and dressed
the bullfrog in a satin vest;

who went to school in pinafores
and named her love by apple cores.

The dollhouse underneath the vine,
the acorn dishes—Mother's? Mine?

Impossible to tear asunder
these childhoods interlaced with wonder!

LAMBING SEASON

That special morning we would start out early,
The March sun dazzling on the frozen crust
But not yet warm, the little white clouds curly
As sheeps' wool; buckets by the path might hold
An inch of maple sap, sweet, icy, thin,
Spring's own taste.
                    Finding Grandpa, we'd go in
The great barn, dim and shadowy and cold,
To see the new lambs just a few hours old,
To share the hearty welcome—ewes all bleating,
Unsteady black-faced babies round their mothers,
Crowding and nuzzling. (Always there'd be one
To carry home, one weaker than the others
To feed from bottles, cradle by the stove,
Cosset and love.)
                    And that was spring—old trees
Leaved out with buckets, curious chickadees
And screaming jays, a fleecy bundle snug
In Grandpa's arms—the lovely sum of these.

BELATED THANK YOU NOTE

No satin gown, no velvet or brocade,
outwears in memory that simple one
of rosebud-patterned dimity you made,
working till midnight so it could be done
for a last day of school—old doors all through
wide to the summer dark, moths on the screen
lamplight across your brown hair as I'd lean
watching, possessed by eeriness, we two
awake in a still house! The whirring treadle
raced on until at last you stopped the needle,
smiled, pushed your curls back, holding up a dress
cut out of love and stitched with tenderness.

BLOOD-DEEP, BONE-DEEP

If my eyes fail,
my feet will know their way
across old floors, the need for caution where
the kitchen runs downhill, its timbers sagging;
a circuit through the chambers' dark zigzagging;
I shall not need to count the bottom stair
going down cellar,
since my feet are sure.

Chair-bound,
my ears could tell dry vines which tap
October fingers on a certain pane;
a rush that's attic mouse or chimney swallow;
which eaves are running with a southeast rain.—
The creaking sighs of one old bench that follow
its unseen occupant
my heart would know.

THE LANTERN

Supper dishes finished,
Gram went making calls
eager for some gossip;
bundled up in shawls,
mittens, fascinator,
against the evening chill;
carrying a lantern
to light her down the hill.

When it came eight-thirty,
we'd begin to pass
casually on errands
which took us by the glass,
watching for a distant
glimmer.
Now and then
a star looks like that lantern
coming home again.

Set in Goudy light Old Style, a delicately-styled original alphabet drawn by the American designer Frederic W. Goudy for the Monotype in 1905. Printed on Hallmark Eggshell Book paper. Designed by William Gilmore.